A Messag

This book introduces common business practices and topics that you will need to get started on your entrepreneurial journey. That journey will not be easy, but it will be worth it. Follow your dreams and never allow anyone to steal the passion of your journey!

**ISBN:** 978-0-692-87089-1

Printed in the U.S.A.
First issued in November 2016

# Table of Contents

## All You Need is an Idea

It was a typical Saturday afternoon. Maya Santiago and her best friend, Sasha Williams, were walking through the mall chatting and window-shopping. But this visit to the mall seemed a little off. Whenever Sasha saw a cute outfit in the display window, she squealed with joy and would drag Maya into the store. For some reason, Maya wasn't enjoying herself. She wanted to buy cute clothes that she saw, but she didn't have the money to spend. This turned her usual cheerful mood gloomy.

"Look Maya! Look at that dress in the window. It looks so pretty; it matches my shoes perfectly." Sasha said. But Maya did not answer. They walked past the store and over to the food court. "Maya! Maya! You are not saying a word. Are you OK?" she continued as they walked to the pretzel stand.

Counting her cash and realizing she only had enough for a drink, Maya shook her head. Sasha knew her girl and didn't want to push it, but she couldn't let it go. Sitting down, Sasha eyed the small drink Maya bought and asked her what was wrong.

Maya sighed "This isn't fun, Sasha" she said looking down.

She explained to Sasha how her mother struggled to pay the bills. Making rent each month had been hard lately. If that wasn't enough, her little brother George went to the hospital again because of problems with his weak immune system.

"I don't want to be another burden to her, Sasha. I want to help her, but I can't even get a job!" Maya blurted all in one breath.

Sasha nodded and said, "Girl, I get it. You are a strong and hardworking lady. Have you thought about being an entrepreneur? Have you ever thought of owning your own business?"

Maya looked at her as if she'd grown two heads, four eyes and sprouted green hair. "I don't have money to invest in a business, let alone any money to risk." Maya said sadly.

Sasha placed a hand on Maya's arm and explained that being a business tycoon wasn't about just investing and risking money. "An entrepreneur is someone who can take any idea, a product, or service and have the skills, will, and courage to turn those ideas into a successful business," she explained. "And you have these qualities" she continued.

Now Maya was intrigued and wanted to know how. Sasha smiled and said, "First you have to set a goal."

While they threw away their trash and walked out of the food court, Maya asked, "Could helping my mother's financial struggle be considered a goal?"

Sasha nodded, "Sure, becoming a little more financially independent is a good goal."

Maya smiled, thinking of what she could do. She stopped suddenly and blurted, "Now you know I don't have any skills, right?"

Sasha laughed and pulled Maya into a tiny, yet lovely store filled with jewelry displays and fashionable clothing. Once inside, she faced Maya and said, "Sure you do."

Maya shook her head in dismay as they walked to the counter, where a woman greeted them with a warm smile. The woman seemed to be expecting Sasha when the girls reached the counter. She told Sasha that all of Sasha's bracelets had sold out just before handing Sasha an envelope filled with money. Thanking the shop keeper,

Sasha took the money and deposited it into her purse. She pulled out a tube of colorful bracelets and gave them to the shopkeeper.

The three talked for nearly 30 minutes. Sasha explained to Maya that the shop keeper, Mrs. Harris, was a friend of her mother's who had offered to help Sasha with the sale of her bracelets. "Maya is thinking of becoming an entrepreneur too, but she thinks she has no skills." Sasha told Mrs. Harris.

Mrs. Harris asked Maya if there was something she was good at and loved doing. Maya shrugged as she knew she wasn't good at arts and crafts or fashion or computers. "You are great at baking cookies Maya," Sasha reminded her. Mrs. Harris felt that baking was a great skill.

Maya thought of this and considered the chance of selling cookies and pastries. She enjoyed baking, but would she enjoy it as much once it was for money? For the remainder of the weekend, Maya thought about the idea of selling cookies and being able to help her mother a bit, even if only by supporting herself financially a little more.

That Monday, she walked into class and with a huge smile told Sasha that she made up her mind to do it. Sasha jumped up and hugged Maya tightly. They planned to debut Maya's cookies during their classroom's upcoming fundraising cookout.

Maya, excited with the prospect of starting her own business, spent most of the week baking cookies and writing down a few goals. She made a huge poster and hung it in the wall of her room to remind her of her goals. In her diary, she wrote about her vision plan and created a list of short-term goals. With all of this, Maya still had doubts regarding the success of her idea, but she was ready to give it a try.

During the cookout, Maya set up her cookie stand. Sasha volunteered to walk around offering free samples. Many students and families stopped by Maya's stand, but only a few made any purchases. Gradually, Maya's excitement started fading as the day went on. She thought her cookies would have been a huge success, but they were not. As they began to clean up at the end of the cookout, she told Sasha that this might not be for her.

"Nonsense, you had a great start!" Sasha protested and added, "Things won't take off right away. There will be good days and bad days, failures and risk taking, but you can learn from each of them." Maya considered this and nodded, a slight smile tugging at her lips.

The following day, she asked her grandmother, Grandma Eva, if she could take cookies to church, or perhaps offer some to either her prayer group or book club. Her grandmother didn't hesitate to say yes.

For a couple of days, Maya spent her time at the school's library doing research on what it takes to be an entrepreneur and starting a small business. She found some helpful tips, such as the importance of setting both short-term and long-term goals. She read about setting realistic goals and to avoid reaching for the clouds right away.

Maya was fascinated by the amount of information there was for new entrepreneurs. She also read some articles online where the authors spoke about the importance of researching the market and scoping out the competition. Taking that advice to heart, Maya researched gourmet cookie products and cookie shops in her town. She wanted to see what other businesses were offering.

Maya planned to sell something unique that would set her apart from the competition. She hoped by doing so, she would stand out and make her business a success. She became excited about her new business.

"I got some special cookie orders for you!" her grandmother announced quickly. It was the middle of the week and Maya knew she had to stay on top of things to deliver the orders in time.

Feeling excited, Maya hugged her grandmother and dove right into the baking process. She made sure she had all the ingredients to bake each type of cookie. Unfortunately, she quickly realized that she had to give up a lot of her free time to bake cookies and fulfill orders. Half of the cookies were for her grandmother's book club meeting on Saturday afternoon and the other half were going to a prayer group that met on Sunday.

Maya's excitement was quickly disappearing when she couldn't go to the movies with Sasha on Friday night or to her cousin's baseball game on Saturday.

"Why so sad?" her mother asked that Saturday morning.

When Maya explained how she felt, her mother hugged her and said, "With everything in life there are pros and cons. You have to consider each one of them thoroughly and decide if the benefits outweigh the rest."

Maya thought about her mother's advice. While the last batch of cookies baked, she took out a sheet of paper and started writing down the pros and cons of entrepreneurship.

Entrepreneurship gave Maya plenty of flexibility. She could work whenever she had the time. It also meant that she would have to give up some of her social activities and learn to manage her time better to do the things she enjoyed and keep up with school work.

Being an entrepreneur also meant she would have to make all the decisions and find solutions to problems that could result from her decisions. Since she was the owner of the business, she would be responsible for every aspect of its growth or failure.

Maya looked back at the past few weeks and realized that becoming an entrepreneur was truly exciting. She came up with an idea, set up some goals, and even put her business in motion. It was all exhilarating. But she was also aware that there would always be risks. Looking down at her list, Maya laughed because she knew the benefits outweighed the disadvantages.

The oven dinged and, with a bounce in her step, Maya took out the cookies to let them cool. She carefully placed them on a container and they were ready to go. Her entire family had been very supportive from the start, which motivated Maya even more.

That evening, after Maya had made her last delivery, she went to her room and counted the money from her cookie sales. The money wasn't a huge amount, but she was happy with it.

Suddenly Maya had an idea. She thought about how hard things were for her mother and really wanted to help. She thought about one of her primary goals for the business and knew what she had to do. Maya found an envelope and placed all the profits inside of it. She waited till everyone was asleep and then tip-toed to her mother's bedroom door.

Maya leaned down and slid the envelope through the door slit into her mother's room and smiled proudly.

The next morning, she woke up to her tearful mother, who held the envelope to her chest.

Hugging Maya, she said, "Thank you honey, but I can't take all of your earned money."

Kissing her mother's cheek, Maya said, "I did it to help you, momma, so please take it."

Unable to refuse Maya's kind offer, her mother took the money, all the while thanking her sweet baby girl.

Maya felt truly pleased for being able to help her mother. She decided to give her business her best efforts. She named her business 'Maya's Homely Gourmet Cookies.'

Maya's cousin, Manny, was a website designer. She asked him for help in promoting her business. Within weeks, Maya had a website and social media accounts set up for her business.

With the help of Sasha and Mrs. Harris, they spread the word about Maya's cookies. Soon enough, business started moving in the right direction. Little by little, Maya helped her mother with the bills, had some money for shopping, and even started a savings account at the local bank. Even when orders were slow, Maya didn't give up. She learned from past mistakes and the failures of other entrepreneurs. Maya was now an entrepreneur and excited about the many opportunities ahead of her.

## It Starts With the Cookies

Maya enjoyed running her own business. Things were going well after a rocky start. People in her community began noticing that Maya was serious about her business. Rumors swirled about how good her cookies were and new customers began rolling in. She was truly grateful for the support of her family and friends. She could count on them to spread the word of Homely Gourmet Cookies.

Maya was so pleased to see her business growing. She never imagined how far she would have come, or having this much success so quickly. However, she knew that there was still a lot to be learned when it came to owning a business.

For starters, Maya needed to perfect her product. She knew her cookies were tasty, but they needed some work to stand out. Maya decided to work on her product. She also wanted some new variations that didn't already exist in her local market.

Maya's first step was to scope out the competition and sample their products. Accompanied by her best friend, Sasha, Maya visited the local bakeries and gourmet cookie shops in town.

At each shop, Maya asked if they offered a sample platter. If they did, Sasha and she compared the different selections. They took notes on how the cookies tasted. They also noted which types of cookies would appeal to her clientele, such as the older ladies in her grandmother's book club and prayer group.

Scoping the market took Maya the better part of a month, but it was worth it. She understood what her competitors offered, their range of choices, and what their most popular products were.

"For my cookies to stand out, I want to offer something unique," she told Sasha.

"Gourmet cookies with a taste of home," she discussed with her mother one evening while baking a batch of cookies.

"That's an interesting idea," her mother thought aloud. "How will you blend the flavor of a gourmet product with a touch of hominess?"

Maya thought of her mother's question. She would have to try out different mixes to get the flavor combinations right. This latest challenge excited her a lot.

Maya loved trying new recipes with different cooking ingredients. She would mix old and new to bring out brand new flavors. Maya worked with her original cookie recipes and mixed in new items to come up with her vision of a unique flavor. She did this several different ways.

Throughout the week, Maya searched new recipes on the internet. She looked for gourmet cookie recipes and ways to bake them that would change their texture and flavor. She found several tips and suggestions on how to make gourmet cookies stand out by making them taste like something grandma would make and not something that was manufactured in a factory.

"It's the weekend!" Maya announced to herself. She was eager to buy the ingredients she would need for her next attempt at perfecting her cookie recipes. She couldn't wait to try the recipes she found on the internet.

Getting every ingredient was important. However, the costs of some ingredients were greater than what she expected. She would have to address that issue too, but that could come once she perfected the recipes.

Maya wasted no time at all. As soon as she got home, she went straight to the kitchen to start mixing. After combining ingredients, the baking got started! She decided to make only half a batch on her first attempt in case she didn't get the mixes right. This way, she would still have ingredients left for another batch.

"This tastes awful!" Maya said around a mouth full of cookie. Her first batch of cookies tasted doughy and was low in sugar. The texture and color of the cookie after baking wasn't right either. She decided to try again. But this time she would use different ingredients.

She baked some cookies with brown sugar and others with white sugar. One batch was made with organic ingredients and the other was baked with non-organic ingredients. It was also important to Maya that the ingredients were commonly found in most stores so that she wouldn't have problems purchasing supplies.

The outcome of the second batch was better and this made Maya happy. The batch of cookies she made with brown sugar had a rich golden color, smelled great and looked incredibly yummy. When Maya tasted it, she knew instantly this was the winning combination.  "OMG!" thought Maya. "This cookie will hit!"

The batch she baked with white sugar and regular store ingredients tasted good, too. The cookies looked scrumptious and smelled delicious, but their coloring was a bit off. They weren't as golden as the brown sugar cookies. She would consider this issue later.

For the remainder of the week, Maya tried different mixes until she felt like it was perfect. She wanted her product to scream the message 'gourmet cookies with a hint of hominess.'

But Maya was still far from perfecting her product. She still needed to consider the cost of ingredients and what her clients' most popular requests were. She needed to consider her customers and make cookies that would sell to her target market.

Maya considered vegans. Then she thought about people with nut allergies, the health-conscious customers, and, especially, the elderly. And since a lot of her clients were elderly ladies from her grandmother's church group and book club, she needed to consider issues like diabetes. Maya sighed and rubbed her forehead. She had so many things to consider. She started feeling somewhat overwhelmed.

"Take it one step at a time," her mother suggested. "You need to figure out how to obtain cost-effective ingredients without sacrificing the quality of your cookies or spending all of your profit on them."

Maya nodded slightly. "How about customer preferences?" "Customers' preference could come after you have figured out a cost-effective way to purchase the ingredients." her mother said.

The next weekend, Maya joined her mother for the weekly grocery shopping trip. She took with her a list of ingredients she needed. As she shopped, she compared prices. Maya found out that brown sugar was more expensive than white sugar. Organic ingredients tended to be on the expensive side also. But vegan ingredients, like white sugar and lactose substitutes, were affordable.

Maya's grandmother listened to Maya retell the story of her findings at the supermarket. She told Maya that if she wanted to cut costs to consider buying ingredients at the local farmers' market. Maya gave her grandmother a curious look.

"For real? Same quality at a lower price?" Maya questioned.

"Yes, Maya," Grandma Eva replied. "The farmers' market is a place local farmers sell products like eggs, milk, fruits, and nuts. At times, even freshly made butter is sold at a lower price than that of the supermarkets."

Maya considered what her grandmother had said. The next weekend, she visited the farmers' market with her Grandma Eva. She was shocked to find a lot of her ingredients there, even flour.

Later that day, Maya discovered how rich the flavor of the cookies was even after switching the brown sugar out for white sugar. She remembered from her research that with a few drops of honey or molasses, she could keep the same amount of sweetness without changing the general flavor profile.

By buying at the farmers' market and at the supermarket, Maya could cut back on the cost of ingredients. Also, based on some tips she found online, she discovered new ways to make her flavors stand out even more without being overwhelming. She wanted her customers to remember her cookies. Maya didn't want her cookies to be just another option, but rather the preferred option.

These thoughts brought Maya to the next step of perfecting her product. She thought about which of her cookies were in high demand. For the next couple of weeks, Maya kept track of the cookie orders she received. She took note of the cookies her customers liked most and how frequently she received orders from those customers. Maya made a chart and hung it on the fridge. Whenever she received a new order, she wrote it down in the chart.

After two weeks, Maya took the chart, walked to the dinner table and studied it. She noticed that a lot of people ordered her classic chocolate chip cookies with a twist. Her triple chocolate cookies, white chocolate cookies, macadamia nut cookies and thumb print cookies were among the most popular. This made Maya happy because most of these cookies used a lot of the same ingredients. There were only a few exceptions like white chocolate or nuts.

Maya was pleased, but her task was far from over. As she had expected, lots of the orders were for sugar-free and vegan cookies. Also, a significant number of requests for low sugar and fat-free cookies came in from customers with diabetes. These were the orders she needed to pay special attention to because a mistake could result in serious health issues. Maya didn't want her grandmother to suffer with high sugar because of a mistake she made with her cookies, nor put her lactose intolerant customers in danger either.

Maya spent every second of her spare time perfecting her mixes for her special group of customers. She was a firm believer in everyone being able to enjoy a tasty cookie, regardless of their health problems and was determined to make it happen. However, she was still struggling with the ratio of artificial sweetener and lactose replacements.

"I knew coming up with a unique flavor profile would take a lot of hard work, but had no idea how much more challenging it would get," Maya commented to Sasha one day during their lunch break.

Sasha understood well how Maya felt having helped her parents at their restaurant with similar issues. She knew it might be a real challenge to get the proportions right. "Perhaps you shouldn't focus as much on one product that satisfies all, but on a couple of variations of the same product," Sasha advised. "You can have a line of cookies for the general market and a line of cookies specifically for customers with health concerns," she continued.

Maya took a few moments and nodded. Sasha was right. She felt pressured to give her special customers the same tasty cookies as everyone else, but her thoughts began to muddle up by her constant fears of getting the mixtures wrong and putting someone's health in danger. She needed to first get a great product together. Then she could create a variation of the same product and people would know that Homely Gourmet Cookies cared enough to offer them a special line of products.

Maya tried her best to relax and just enjoy the baking process. She set off to baking again. Perfecting a product was much harder than they made it look online, but it was all part of being a successful entrepreneur.

After baking another batch, Maya laughed with joy as the cookies had turned out as she expected. She still had to work out some texture issues, but the flavor was right on.

"Grandma Eva, try this please!" Maya eagerly said to Grandma Eva before the cookie had even cooled off.

Her grandmother took the cookie and a smile appeared on her lips. The smell alone was enough to make her mouth water. A bite of the cookie and her taste buds were delighted.

"This is so good!" she said with a smile.

Maya's smile grew bigger. She knew that if her grandmother liked the cookie, others would too. But feedback from others was very important. She gave the rest of the cookies to her grandmother to share with her friends. Maya asked her to please give them to the book club ladies and to let her know what they thought.

Feedback is crucial for perfecting a product; Maya remembered reading that online. She would encourage her customers to give honest feedback. Maya understood that not all the feedback she would get would be positive, but she was ready to hear it. Any negative comments could be used as a tool to improve her product.

A few days passed and Maya started getting feedback from her special customers as well as her regulars. Everyone loved the cookies for the most part, but some were concerned with appearance and texture. This information was helpful. She knew that getting the mix right wouldn't happen overnight, but she was a step closer to perfecting her product.

Over time, Maya came up with her ideal product and flavor profile that would set her cookies apart from the rest of the local bakeries. Sasha's parents, Mr. and Mrs. Williams, also helped by loaning Maya some of the kitchen area from time to time, including the industrial oven. Maya learned a lot about baking from them and was more than glad to offer her customers better cookies.

Taking the time to perfect her product paid off in a huge way. Maya's cookies were tastier than ever and her business grew steadily. Her regular customers continued buying cookies from her. Word of mouth from customers to their friends brought in new patrons. Everyone wanted to try out the gourmet product with a touch of hominess.

## Maya Spreads the Word

Throughout the holidays, a steady stream of orders poured in for Homely Gourmet Cookies. Maya's business had built a solid customer base. This kept the business afloat. Most of Maya's clients now enjoy ordering cookies as gifts for their loved ones. Maya had steady sales and the business ran strong through Christmas. However, following the holidays, Maya saw a huge dip in orders as business slowed down notably.

This situation didn't bother Maya as she had read a lot about this and the challenges that impacted consumable products. She had predicted that sales would drop based on her research into consumer trends. She had also spoken to Mrs. Harris and learned that in the first few months of a new year, most businesses that sold consumer products were slow. However, she knew that Valentine's Day was one of the few opportunities to make up sales during the beginning of the year.

"How can I compensate for those slow times?" Maya asked Mrs. Harris one afternoon. The shopkeeper smiled and said, "I make sure to increase my awareness, come up with new deals and incentives that will motivate my buyers and attract new ones. That is my secret," she said, giving Maya a wink.

Maya had never thought of implementing marketing as a tool to promote her business. She didn't realize that marketing had a lot of benefits besides just getting the word out to people.

That evening, when she got home, she powered up her computer and did some research on the long-term benefits of marketing. Her goal was to identify different ways she could market her cookies without blowing her budget. "Amazing," Maya whispered to herself. She read that marketing is a powerful force for a successful business because it can be used to entice new customers, spread the word about products, and help encourage repeat business.

Valentine's Day was quickly approaching, so she thought it was a perfect time to test out some strategies. Maya looked through her past order log files. She took notes on who were her frequent buyers, occasional buyers and rare buyers. She also took notes of their age groups and the cookies they preferred buying. Maya decided to use all the information to come up with a marketing plan.

Sadly, Maya found it challenging coming up with a good strategy. She read about different marketing strategies and how to deliver the right message to potential customers, but she couldn't decide which method was best for her. She found an article online that mentioned the three I's of marketing: Inquire, Inform, and Inspire.

Maya figured out that she needed to first inquire what her customers liked about her business and her products. She wanted to know what made them come back for more of her cookies and how they felt about how she was running her business. She wanted to hear about what they liked and disliked.

Maya listed her most frequent customers. She dedicated the next couple of days to sending some e-mails, giving some a call, or stopping by for a quick visit. She was pleased to receive a lot of feedback. Customers wanted to share their opinion and Maya welcomed all of it.

With this information in hand, Maya began to study the competition. She compared information she received from her customers with online reviews. She also asked coffee shop and bakery shop owners that she worked with about their feelings on her competitors. Not every cafe and bakery owner was willing to share information, but she gathered enough insight to form a strong marketing message. Maya also took notice of the ways those businesses marketed their products and the unique promotions they had in effect to increase their orders.

For the most part, Maya's competitors used a mix of consistent, informative and direct marketing to get their messages across. Maya saw the value in this, but wasn't convinced on which way she should market her products to her customers. She wanted to understand how customers connected with her business. Did her cookies inspire people? Were her customers simply connected to her and wanted to support her? Was there a story that motivated customers to consider trying out her cookies and buy them over the competition? She rubbed her forehead tiredly and sighed, pushing the laptop aside.

"Something wrong?" her mother questioned as she walked by with a basket of clothes to iron.

"I can't figure out the inspiring aspect of my cookies." Maya grumbled.

As her mother pulled out the ironing board from the closet, she thought of the question for a few seconds.

"There are lots of inspiring things that have come from your business," she responded.

Maya tilted her head, "Like what?"

"Your drive to sell the cookies to help pay the bills has been an inspiration for me," she said. "You also have inspired others to try their best and try their luck with something they hadn't thought of before. And I am sure you have inspired Sasha in trying new ways of doing the same thing." she said before starting to iron.

Maya thought for a moment. "Perhaps I should ask for testimonials from buyers, of how my cookies have inspired them, or what they find adorable about them," she said.

"That's a great idea," her mother said, knowing firsthand the positive effect on those who had helped with the business.

Acting on her thoughts, Maya reached out to people again to find out what connected them to her products and whether they were inspired by Homely Gourmet Cookies. She was surprised to read and hear that her products had affected their lives. Folks commented on how her business served as an example for young people who wanted to earn their own money. Several people thought it was admirable that she wanted to raise money to help support her family. Others commented on how thoughtful she was with her ingredients in certain cookies tailored to folks with food restrictions. Maya had no idea that she was a role model for those near to her and even other children in her community.

After so much hard work, Maya got an answer to her marketing message and strategy. Instead of using one form to deliver her marketing message, she would use a mix of consistent and direct marketing. Maya was aware that to make these marketing strategies work, she would have to keep in touch with her customers and stay updated on innovative strategies and techniques.

With the help of her cousin, Manny, she was confident she could keep on top of marketing. When she presented her ideas to

Manny, he asked, "Where do you want to market and sell your cookies?"

"I haven't thought of that," she told Manny. "With my small budget, I can't afford to throw a lot of money into a marketing campaign that may or may not work."

"Take a hard look at your customer base Maya" Manny suggested. He told her to look at her most frequent buyers and who those people were. "Just like you had done while figuring out your marketing and advertising methods," he further explained.

Most of Maya's customers were students, working class parents and the elderly. She had some special requests for community event organizers. There were rare orders for social events like parties, corporate events and weddings, but those were the least frequent. Taking those aspects into reflection, Maya figured out what the best marketing methods for those people would be, and where she could sell and advertise her cookies in a way that could catch their attention.

"I can advertise and market my cookies through social media. I can also advertise at my school clubs, school functions, and at community events," Maya told Manny.

"Those are all good ideas. But you may also want to consider advertising outside the box," said Manny. He encouraged her to think of places where her cookies will stand out. He used examples of advertising her cookies at the arts and crafts shows, the local music festivals, and even comic conventions.

Maya nodded in agreement, but that still didn't answer the question of how she could advertise her cookies without blowing her budget on ad campaigns. Again, Maya rushed to her laptop, flung it open and started surfing the net on how to cut costs on marketing. Maya found a blog post about business tycoons who advertised their products with a very low budget.

"The best way to advertise my cookies on a small budget would be by word of mouth" she said to herself. She also decided to use her already owned social media network to spread the word of her cookies. She would also create special promotions, unique content and incentives for people to notice her products. Maya would also create fliers to place at school, the local supermarket stores and even at Mrs. Harris' shop in the mall. Her fliers would introduce her products to new customers and help spread the word of her business.

Sasha suggested one afternoon that she should create some enticing stories. The stories would tell why her cookies stood out from the rest and why people kept coming back. She should tell a story about her cookies' unique homely taste to make buyers feel nostalgic for those days of being a child and eating fresh, homemade cookies that drew you in with the smell from the oven. By engaging her customers' senses, through storytelling, Maya could drive even more customers to her business.

Maya took Manny's advice of advertising her cookies in places where they would likely stand out. With the help of some of her friends, Maya got access to the music festival, a few of the arts and crafts expos, the local farmers' market, and the annual comic book convention. Maya prepared unique cookies with special molds and designs for these events.

Her marketing delivered a message about how her cookies consider the health of her customers. She wanted potential buyers to know that she considered them when she made her cookies by not cutting corners on the quality of ingredients and working diligently on flavor profiles. She wanted people to know that she built her business the right way and for the right reasons. Maya also wanted people to know that she believed in her product and offered discounted prices that welcomed new customers.

When Valentine's Day rolled around, there had been a significant increase in the number of orders that came in. She even rolled out a new cookie just for Valentine's Day: The Valentine Bliss, a raspberry-infused chocolate chip cookie. She felt that this would be a one-of-a-kind cookie flavor that her competitors hadn't considered.

Maya knew that as her business grew, her marketing strategy would have to expand as well. What was important to her was that she remained true to her message, and that she never stopped listening to the feedback from her customers and the market. If she stuck to this strategy, she knew that she would be just fine.

## Finding Purpose in Baking

Homely Gourmet Cookies was quickly becoming a staple of the community. Maya's recipes included quality ingredients. Customers didn't only appreciate her, but loved that she took such care in preparing cookies for different types of customers.

Summer was around the corner and cookie orders started to pick up. Her client base had doubled and there were several local events being held over the summer. It would be difficult to keep up demand by herself.

Maya knew that with increased sales, she would have to consider hiring help. She didn't think that finding people would be a problem. With summer coming, she had no doubt that family and friends would be willing to jump in, but she was hesitant to ask for help, or to bring other people into her little business.

Asking for help with promoting her cookies, seeking advice, even with creating a website and social media pages was not the same as asking people to work directly with her in its process. Maya feared that if she brought people to work along with her, her vision for the business would become blurry and she would end up losing sight of her goals and objectives. Maya rubbed her eyes. She let out a frustrated sigh, which caught her mother's attention.

"Something wrong?" her mother asked, concerned.

Frowning, Maya looked at her. "I'm having trouble keeping up with cookie orders, but I'm scared to ask others for help."

Her mother sat beside her, placing a soothing hand on Maya's. She said, "At times, in order to succeed, one must take a risk and ask for help."

Maya explained to her mother her concerns with asking others for help. Her mother saw Maya's concerns as valid ones. She suggested that Maya do some research on it before asking for help. She should list out roles and expectations and determine how the helpers would be compensated.

Hearing those words made Maya feel better. Research had helped her at the starting phase of her business. She reasoned that being well-informed is always a benefit. This would also provide some guidance on growing a business without losing sight of the objectives.

Maya spent some time researching. She studied small business growth challenges and the ups and downs of bringing in people to help. Her first step was to list possible candidates that she thought had the same goals and ideas in mind. Maya thought that perhaps asking people who shared the same views and opinions on her cookie business would be beneficial for her business long-term. She also hoped that by doing so, it wouldn't damage the vision and goals she had for the future of her business.

Her mother, Grandma Eva, her best friend, Sasha, Mrs. Harris, and Sasha's parents were people who had helped her before and might help again. They had all been supportive, so asking them for help would be an easy thing. Maya also considered other like-minded people to help her, in case those in her initial list wouldn't be able to provide the help she would need. After spending most of the evening narrowing down her list of the best candidates, Maya went to sleep peacefully.

The next day, she started out by asking her mother, grandmother and Sasha for help. They were all eager to help Maya with her business. Sasha loved Maya and was excited to help her. Sasha knew that her prior experience as an entrepreneur would bring insight to Homely Gourmet

Cookies. With her influence, Maya's business could be even more successful.

As Maya had predicted, Sasha's parents weren't able to help because of their busy schedule at their family restaurant. However, they continued to offer Maya full access to their industrial kitchen. Mrs. Harris also was busy with her shop. She assured Maya that she would continue to promote the cookie business by handing out fliers to her customers. Maya was more than pleased with their continued support. Maya did enlist the help of three of her other friends; Shay, Sofia, and Gloria. These were people she knew and trusted to work hard.

Memorial Day, the weekend before the school year was over, brought a huge demand of special cookies. Maya could not enjoy the long weekend by going to the pool with her family. She found herself deep in the industrial kitchen baking cookies, finishing all the orders on time.

By mid-Saturday afternoon, Maya was struggling and stressed. She was running behind schedule. There was no way she could fill all the orders in what little time she had left. Maya had initially planned to bring everyone on board the first week of summer. She had also planned to have everyone gather for an unofficial meeting to run through the goals and vision for the business. It was important that everyone was on the same page and working towards the same objective. But being so short in time forced her to throw all those plans out of the window.

Reaching for her cellphone, Maya called in the troops. She felt pleased to see her four friends show up; they were ready to give her a hand on such short notice. Even her cousins, Dana and Linda, came to help with assembling and distributing the cookies. On Memorial Day, Maya had fulfilled every single order request on time. She gave a slight sigh and thanked everyone.

Summer rolled in and as expected, Homely Gourmet Cookies already had a bunch of orders to fill and more were rolling in. Maya's family and friends showed up as planned, ready to help as before. Maya smiled as they stood in front of her. She couldn't be happier to have so many wonderful people willing to help her. She glanced at the chart she had taped to the wall of the industrial kitchen and started explaining what it meant.

Maya had divided her helpers into groups based on their skills and areas of expertise. This was to help with tasks that best suited them. Her mother and grandmother would help with baking the cookies when they had free time. Dana and Linda would help with taking the orders. Shay, Sofia, and Gloria would be responsible for product delivery. She left purchasing of ingredients to Sasha who she knew well and could trust with money.

At first, everyone seemed to take their assigned duties in their stride. For a couple of days, things were smooth. But Maya started picking up on small lapses taking place. At the time, they were insignificant, but she had no doubt those flaws would grow to bigger problems if left alone.

First, it was a variation in ingredients. Different brands were being purchased and ingredients were being bought at a different place than where Maya had specified. All natural butter was replaced by margarine and certain other ingredients were substituted for less expensive alternatives. When Maya asked Sasha, she justified the purchases by explaining her purchases were a better investment and that there was a great sale on margarine she couldn't pass up. Maya had to explain why she chose the ingredients she did and asked Sasha not to buy anything that wasn't on her list.

Two days later, Maya received a call from one of her first customers regarding an order she had recently placed. She complained of price changes and a reduced quantity of cookies in her order. Maya became baffled and quite annoyed at this. She had built her reputation on great quality cookies with a unique hominess at an affordable price, not the other way around. Furthermore, the deliveries were all over the place and some were even done late, which resulted in displeased customers.

Over the course of a week, things were gradually getting out of control. Maya was not happy and knew she needed to do something about it, so she called a meeting. As soon as they gathered, Maya asked, "Do you know what my goal is for Homely Gourmet Cookies?" Maya's question met them with blank stares and puzzled faces, at first. Then everyone started talking at once.

"To sell the best tasting cookies?" someone mumbled.

"Make money to help your family?" another added.

"Beat the competition and become the lead cookie seller in the state?" yet another said. And on they went.

Maya felt sad to hear what they thought were her goals for selling cookies. They couldn't be more wrong. Sasha gently touched her arm while everyone else continued to talk about what they thought was best for Maya's business and how she would benefit the most from it. Maya looked at Sasha with a frown.

Sasha leaned closer and whispered, "Did you ever create a mission statement for your business?"

Maya gasped and opened her eyes wide. She suspected she had forgotten to implement something crucial she had read during her research. Now she knew exactly what that was.

A mission statement, as Maya recalled, was the most crucial aspect of a business. A mission statement was the glue that keeps everyone working towards the same goal and keeping the best interests of the business in mind.

"I forgot." Maya said sorrowfully and Sasha gave her hand a squeeze.

"It's never too late to do so." Sasha murmured and with that the meeting went on. Maya tried to explain the best she could what her vision and goals for the business were and what she hoped to accomplish with her cookie business. But she knew, without a mission statement, it wouldn't be enough. She also needed to create a business plan that outlines the overall goals and how the business will achieve those goals. Her business is fast growing and needed these fundamental pieces to move forward.

For the next couple of days, Maya drafted a few mission statements. She struggled with getting the wording and goals to come through. She did some research and found some very helpful samples, but perhaps the most helpful piece of information she could find were four incredibly useful questions that would allow her to create the perfect mission statement.

1.　What do we as a business do?

2.　How do we do it?

3.　Whom do we do it for?

4.　What value are we bringing to our customers and the market?

These simple four questions were the road map Maya needed to create the perfect mission statement:

*At Homely Gourmet Cookies, we bring you unique gourmet cookies with a hint of home sweet home in every bite. We bake each cookie with love and care, using a special blend of all natural ingredients that give it the perfect hint of hominess. Each cookie is hand crafted and prepared with our customers and their unique needs in mind, so that everyone can enjoy a deliciously tasting cookie regardless of diet or life style choices at an affordable price!*

Maya knew her mission statement still needed some work and polishing. But for the time being, this mission statement would keep everyone focused and working towards the same goal. That way they could avoid future mix ups, pricing issues and differences of opinion.

When everyone showed up the following weekend to help with a large cookie order for a wedding, Maya revealed the mission statement. She was ecstatic to see everyone embracing the mission for Homely Gourmet Cookies. They all agreed with the overall goals Maya had created and assured her that they would work towards those goals.

To ensure things kept flowing smoothly, Maya made a big poster and banner with the mission statement and hung it in the industrial kitchen as well as in the home kitchen. This way, everyone would consider it as they worked. Homely Gourmet Cookies now had a specific purpose that everyone understood.

Maya felt relieved to see things flowing smoothly again. With a mission statement in place, the business was more productive and variances removed. Regardless of how many orders they got, Maya was happy because everyone worked together towards a common goal. While they had their views and opinions, everyone knew to always keep the mission in mind.

## Raising Dough for the Future

With the summer gradually coming to an end, Homely Gourmet Cookies was having a successful year. Maya worked hard to ensure a solid foundation that would allow the company to grow. She had established a mission for her business, she created the ideal cookie recipes for her customers, and she had a great team of people working with her. Maya was happy with her business and the success it had achieved so far.

Maya maintained her business's image through effective marketing. This kept driving the business forward while maintaining her mission. Not every week was successful in terms of cookie sales, but Maya and her team enjoyed how things were going. And the business kept growing.

Fall brought with it a new wave of challenges for Maya. Her little brother George had fallen ill again and landed in the hospital. The treatments he required, coupled with a prolonged hospital stay, left Maya's mother scrambling for money. The health insurance hadn't covered much of the costs. Ms. Santiago struggled to pay for the treatments while maintaining the essentials at home.

Maya rendered the help she could. A lot of the profit she had made with her business went to help her mother. The money was nice, but it just wasn't enough. Thus, Maya started diverting funds to help her mother; both funds from her gained profit and from the capital she had set aside for the business expenses. This left her falling short of meeting her budget. Maya knew this was a bad idea because she had read an article online that said to avoid this very issue. She just didn't feel she had a choice.

Maya struggled with buying enough baking supplies and distributing the cookies. She also had to reduce production notably. This put a lot of customers on a waiting list and some were even turned down.

Maya feared she wouldn't be able to raise enough capital to keep her small business afloat. She would have to abandon the idea after all the effort she and everyone else had put into it. This left her truly sad.

Maya had worked very hard over the last year and her business had grown in exposure. She refused to consider the option of giving everything up. In fact, she decided to dedicate more of her time to her business.

Towards the middle of September, another devastating blow impacted Homely Gourmet Cookies. The industrial kitchen Sasha's parents let her borrow had suffered structural damage by a hurricane and had to close for repairs. Maya's home kitchen wasn't enough; it didn't meet the standards required to produce all the cookies she needed to fulfill orders. Not only that, but using a home kitchen was a health code violation for the sale and distribution of baked goods. She feared someone would realize that she baked her cookies at home and she would have to deal with a hefty fine from the City.

"If things keep going like this, I'll have to stop selling cookies." Maya told Sasha during lunch.

Sasha's eyes widened in surprise. She couldn't believe Maya considered quitting her business just like that. "Have you explored other options?"

Maya gave her a puzzled look. "Other options like what?" she wondered, unsure of what options Sasha referred to.

"Raising capital to keep the business afloat." Sasha suggested.

Seeing the frown on Maya's face, Sasha told Maya the story her parents had shared with her when she started selling bracelets. Sasha's parents had told her about what it took for them to get their restaurant opened and to become successful. Their story motivated Sasha, so she hoped it would do the same for Maya.

"Raising capital allows you to expand your business in ways that should increase sales and profit" Sasha explained. She further explained to Maya that raising capital is not only taking out loans. It's also investing some of her own money, reinvesting business profits, or even asking family and friends for financial help.

Maya listened closely to every word Sasha said. "I have never thought of raising money for my business". "Whenever I think of business capital, what comes to mind is bank loans and investors," she said. Maya had never considered other ways to raise money.

Maya had created a savings account after starting her business. She wasn't sure what her goal was for the money, but she knew she wanted to use it on something important to her. Maya decided to invest some of her savings into the business. Homely Gourmet Cookies was important to her and she was happy with her choice.

She went to the bank with her mother and took out half her savings. Maya put that money to use in her business. She bought the supplies she would need to bake and distribute the cookie orders she had for the upcoming weeks. Her mother also helped her rent a small industrial kitchen for a month. She gave the left over money to her mother to help with her brother's medicines.

Maya knew that, for the time being, this would help her out until she could figure out something else, but she only had a month to come up with more money. She wouldn't be able to afford the industrial kitchen for much longer or continue buying cooking supplies.

Over the next week, Maya researched different ways to raise capital for small businesses like hers. The articles she read explained and highlighted a variety of organizations, like the Small Business Administration, willing to help start-up businesses. There were even a few government programs designed for just this purpose.

Maya wanted to be cautious. She looked at options that were quite accessible to her. Her options included asking friends and family for small loans, donations and gifts, crowdfunding options and, of course, organic growth and investment of her own capital. She carefully researched each of these options to ensure that she got it right. It was important for her to know everything she needed before pitching her idea to her family and friends.

Maya figured she'd already asked many of her family members and friends for help with her business, but asking for a small loan, donation, or gift would be much harder. She thought of many ways to approach them. She came up with a strategy that would detail her goals and where she saw the business in the future. Maya created a presentation that showed her sales and expenses for the last year by month. She wanted to use this information to show that she could make money and pay back any loans that she received.

"Could you please help me organize a small get together at the house on Sunday?" she asked her grandmother as soon as she felt confident enough and ready to face her family and friends. She also invited her close friends, family, and friends of family. She wanted to offer them an opportunity to invest in Homely. Maya didn't know how many of them would show up, but when Sunday evening rolled around, she had a house full of people.

After Sunday dinner, the conversation started. Maya introduced the topic of her cookie business, Homely Gourmet Cookies. Many of her family members had heard of the business and how successful it had become in such a short time. They were all curious to hear from her and how it all started.

Maya indulged them and told the story behind her business and how it had grown. Those who had helped her along the way shared their own views. Maya was careful to avoid sounding too arrogant, or over-reaching. She remembered from one of the articles she read that this was crucial.

Maya then spoke about the current condition of the business. She was honest with everyone and told them about her challenges. She went on to explain how she decided to invest some of her savings into the business and her plan for paying herself back with interest.

"My cookie business means a lot to me," she said to the group. "The profits have allowed me to save money, do fun activities, and, most importantly, contribute to our home," she continued. She talked about how good she felt to help her family during tough times.

As the tears gathered at the corners of her eyes threatened to fall, Maya pulled it back. Blinking fast a few times, she took a deep breath. "I'll do all I can to keep this business going, even investing the rest of my savings," she said, "but it would mean a lot to me if you would help me with a small contribution," continued Maya.

Everyone listened attentively. She began to explain the terms for paying back any money loaned to her and rewards given for those who helped with the business. She was thorough in her presentation. Maya especially impressed her uncle Ronny, who is a lawyer, with the presentation. He was surprised at how professional the presentation was for someone so young and just a novice in business. Uncle Ronny started asking a few questions. He wanted to know how much capital Maya needed and what she intended to do with the money she raised. He was also curious whether she had set short-term and long-term goals for the business. He asked Maya about any risks with loaning her money in case the businesses goals are not reached.

Maya was ready with answers. Her research had prepared her for questions like these. These were family and friends that she cared about and she wanted them to know how important they were to her, so she was honest and thoughtful with her replies. Maya knew that integrity is a key character for any business owner and she valued others' confidence in her integrity. Her goal was to raise enough money to cover expenses for the next six months.

"Have you thought about fundraisers, investors, and crowd funding?" her uncle asked.

"Yes, I have" Maya replied with a nod. "Although I need the capital, I don't think it's at the stage I would consider offering strangers access to my business in return for money." Maya also explained that applying for loans with high interest rates didn't seem like a good idea either.

Maya thought it made sense to start with family and friends. The articles that she read online had suggested this as a first option. Next, she planned to partner with a couple of community groups to sell cookies and raise funds for both them and her. Finally, she told the group that crowdfunding was an option, but she hadn't figured out how she would market the campaign.

"I can help with that!" shouted Manny. Having helped with her website and online presence, he felt confident he knew what she wanted. He also offered to promoting her products more. Setting up a crowdfunding campaign wouldn't be difficult and he believed he could help her raise some money through it.

Maya's grandmother offered to help start fundraisers with her church and the book club. Sasha joined in pitching ideas to have different fundraisers for local community groups and helping to promote the business. The meeting ended with several people offering to help. Maya was excited for Homely Gourmet Cookies.

Within a week, Maya raised almost $4000; her uncle Ronny being the largest contributor of all. He also took some time from his busy schedule to help Maya draft a short and easy to understand investment plan that she could distribute to other potential investors. Along with the investment plan, he included loan agreements. This agreement detailed payback options with estimated payment periods and details about interest rates.

Maya drafted a 'thank you' letter for the money gifted to her by family and friends. This was a way to show her gratitude. Also, Maya wanted to give them some form of compensation and cookies seemed like the best option. So along with those thank you letters, she sent them a special bag of cookies.

Maya decided that for the next six months, she would send those that gave her a gift a monthly report. The report would highlight her goals and the progress toward those goals. This would make them feel like they contributed to something worthwhile.

With the capital raised from family and friends, Maya could rent an industrial kitchen while the restaurant was under construction. She had enough money to maintain supplies and keep the business going.

Her grandmother organized a couple of fundraisers at the church and with her book club. Sasha's parents added a free cookie to every dinner ordered on Friday nights. This was a way to introduce Homely Gourmet Cookies to new customers.

Manny set up a crowdfunding campaign for her on a site called Go-Fund Me. The crowdfunding campaign consumed a lot of Maya's time. She had to keep an active online presence and reach out to groups, people and followers of her different social media accounts to ensure a constant flow of contributors to reach her funding goals. She decided to use a portion of every dollar donated to bake cookies for the homeless in her area. This went over well and helped encourage donors to participate in her campaign.

Shortly before Christmas, Maya reached her crowdfunding goal. Orders were up for the holidays and she couldn't control her excitement. There was enough profit each month to cover expenses. Maya could even start making payments to those who loaned her money. She was thankful for Sasha's suggestions of raising capital and not giving up when things seemed too difficult. Maya knew that Homely Gourmet Cookies was here to stay!

## Glossary Terms

***Business Plan*** refers to a document used by entrepreneurs and investors that outlines how a business will be managed and which strategies will be used to help the business succeed.

***Business Objectives*** are a set of clear and measurable steps that paint a picture of the business's pathway to success.

***Capital*** is the money or resources a business has to buy what it needs to make their products or provide services to the market.

***Entrepreneur*** is someone that creates and operates a business while assuming the financial risk of that business.

***Entrepreneurship*** is all of the activities that go into creating, launching, and growing a business.

***Marketing Communications*** refers to the message and the associated media used by a business to distribute that message to the market.

***Mission Statement*** refers to a statement that captures the purpose of the organization, what it stands for, and its reason for existence.

***Vision Statement*** describes how an entrepreneur wants environment to look in the future and helps guide the organization's decisions to help it arrive at that future state.

The Author: Bruce D. Dunams, DBA

Dr. Bruce Dunams is a well-known strategy consultant that thrives on helping organizations face the many challenges of entrepreneurship. He works with entrepreneurs, small businesses, and not-for-profits all over the world by helping them improve their business knowledge. It has always been a goal for him to realize a strong ecosystem of entrepreneurship that supports more young people of color, especially young women of color, who are often left out of business ownership.

Most importantly, Dr. Dunams is an entrepreneur himself. He understands the many challenges faced by start-ups and small businesses. He believes the key to entrepreneurship is starting early, staying focused, and not being afraid to fail. This book is for our aspiring youth. Dr. Dunams wants these entrepreneurs to have the resources and insight they need to make their journey a little easier. This book is his dedication to the next generation of entrepreneurs.

Made in the USA
Monee, IL
06 May 2023

32992157R00036